About This Book

Title: *Trains All Day*

Step: 5

Word Count: 166

Skills in Focus: Long vowel a spelled ai and ay

Tricky Words: cars, water, carry, people, person, every, underground, oil, wood

Ideas For Using This Book

Before Reading:
- **Comprehension:** Look at the title and cover image together. Walk through the pictures in the book with readers and have them make predictions about what they might learn in the book. Help them make connections by asking what they already know about trains.
- **Accuracy:** Practice saying the tricky words listed on page 1.
- **Phonics:** Tell students they will read words with long vowel teams. Explain that *ai* and *ay* make the long vowel sound /a/. Have students look at the title of this book, *Trains All Day*. Ask readers to point to the vowel teams in the title. Help them practice blending the sounds in *trains* and *day*. Have students take a quick look through the first few pages of text to identify and decode additional words with *ai* and *ay* vowel teams, including *contain, rain, may, day, rail,* and *hay*.

During Reading:
- Have readers point under each word as they read it.
- **Decoding:** If readers are stuck on a word, help them say each sound and blend the sounds together smoothly. Be sure to point out words with *ai* and *ay* vowel teams as they appear.
- **Comprehension:** Invite readers to talk about new things they are learning about trains while reading. What are they learning that they didn't know before?

After Reading:
Discuss the book. Some ideas for questions:
- Have you ever ridden on a train? If not, would you like to?
- What do you still wonder about trains?

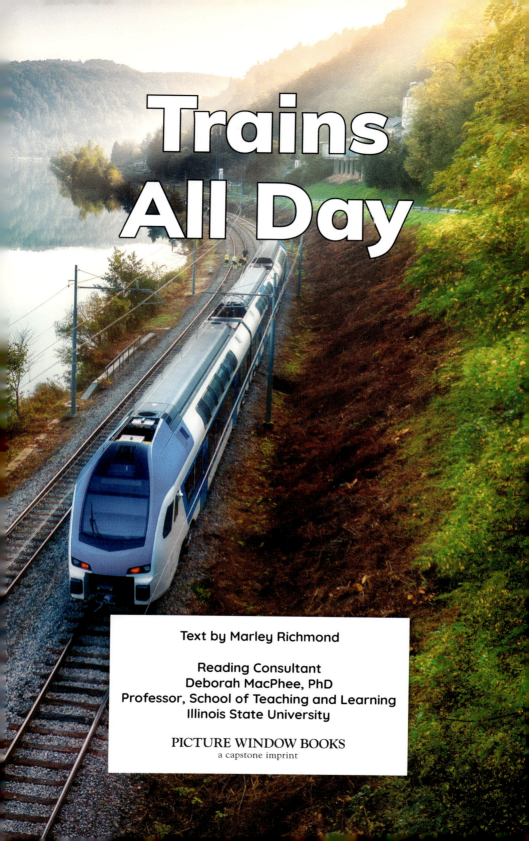

Trains All Day

Text by Marley Richmond

Reading Consultant
Deborah MacPhee, PhD
Professor, School of Teaching and Learning
Illinois State University

PICTURE WINDOW BOOKS
a capstone imprint

Trains run all day and night.

Trains may run
in the sun or rain.

Trains run on rails.
The rails make tracks.

These tracks are railroads.

Some trains run outside.

Some trains run underground.

Trains carry many things.

Trains may carry coal, wood, or grain.

Some trains carry hay.

Some train cars have tanks. They may contain oil or water.

People must pay to ride on trains.

A person can ride a train a very long way.

The train will make stops along the way.

The ride may take a few days.

Some trains have cars with beds. People may sleep in train cars.

People may take the same train every day.

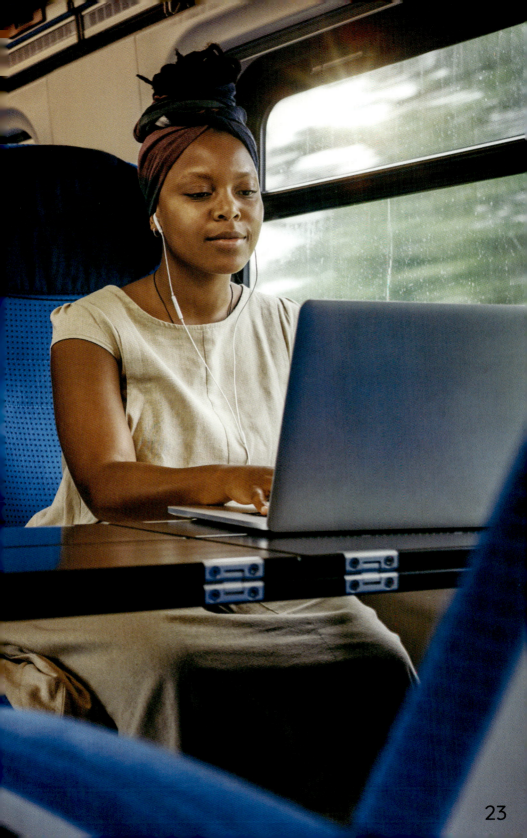

Trains take many people to their jobs each day.

Many trains are plain.

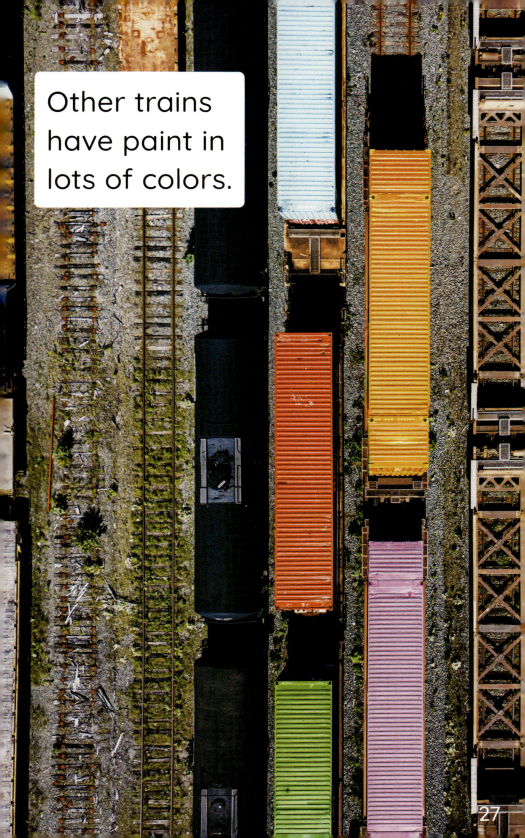
Other trains have paint in lots of colors.

People may play with toy trains.

They can place tracks for the trains.

Trains have lots of jobs.

Trains take people and goods a long way.

More Ideas:

Phonics and Phonemic Awareness Activity

Practicing Vowel Teams:
Play I Spy! Prepare word cards with vowel team story words. Place each card face up on a surface. Choose a word to start the game. Say "I spy" and then break apart the sounds in the word. For example, "I spy /t/, /r/, /a/, /n/." The readers will call out the word and then look for the corresponding card. Continue until all cards have been collected.

Suggested words:
- contain
- rain
- may
- way
- day
- rail

Extended Learning Activity

Play Pretend:
Ask readers to pretend they are taking a train ride. Where are they going? What do they need to bring on their trip? What do they see out the windows of the train? Ask readers to write a short story about their train ride. Challenge readers to use words with long vowel teams, especially *ai* and *ay* words.

Published by Picture Window Books, an imprint of Capstone
1710 Roe Crest Drive, North Mankato, Minnesota 56003
capstonepub.com

Copyright © 2026 by Capstone.
All rights reserved. No part of this publication may be reproduced in whole or in part, or stored in a retrieval system, or transmitted in any form or by any means, electronic, mechanical, photocopying, recording, or otherwise, without written permission of the publisher.

Library of Congress Cataloging-in-Publication Data is available on the Library of Congress website.

ISBN: 9798875227189 (hardback)
ISBN: 9798875230851 (paperback)
ISBN: 9798875230837 (eBook PDF)

Image Credits: iStock: AlenaPaulus, 28–29, Imgorthand, 14, LeoPatrizi, 18–19, mapodile, 22–23, Meinzahn, 26, milehightraveler, 12–13, shaunl, 27, SolStock, 16–17, traveler1116, 10–11, zkolra, 15; Shutterstock: AaronChenPS2, 4, Bjorn Keith, 5, Chaitawat.P, 20–21, Denis Belitsky, 1, 2–3, 24–25, Eddie J. Rodriquez, 9, eFlexion, 30–31, i viewfinder, cover, Jane Rix, 8, 32, Leon Woods, 6–7